EXPERIMENT EARTH

Different UFO's and Phenomenon Across America

Billy Stinnett

To order additional copies of this book, contact:
Xlibris
844-714-8691
www.Xlibris.com
Orders@Xlibris.com

Library of Congress Control Number: 2024902097
ISBN: Softcover   979-8-3694-1571-9
        EBook   979-8-3694-1570-2

Print information available on the last page

Rev. date: 01/31/2024

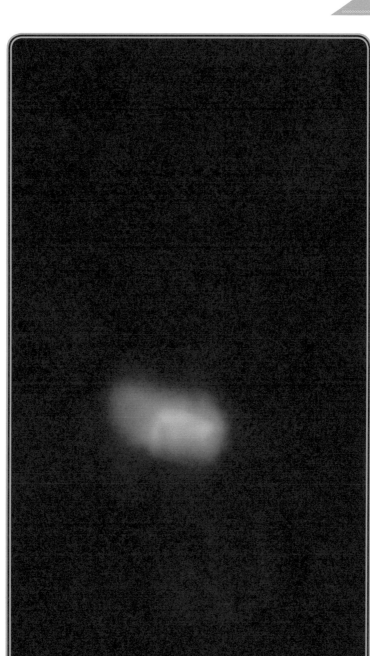

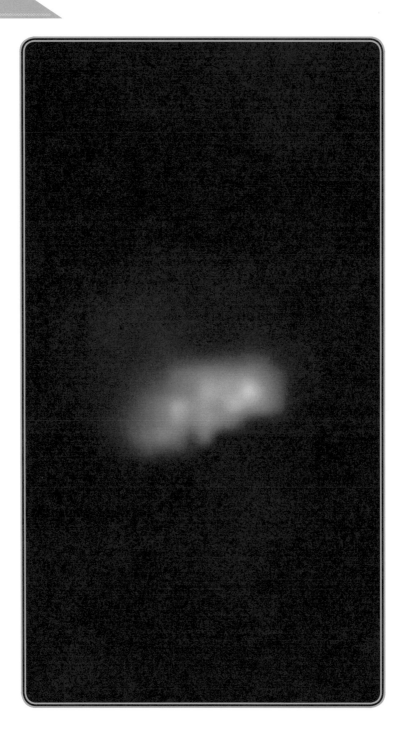

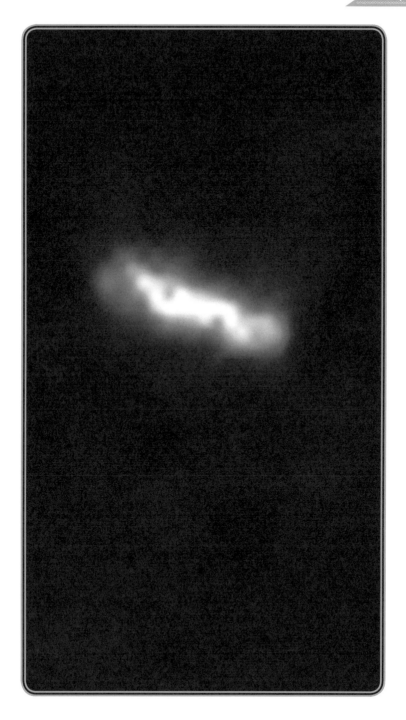

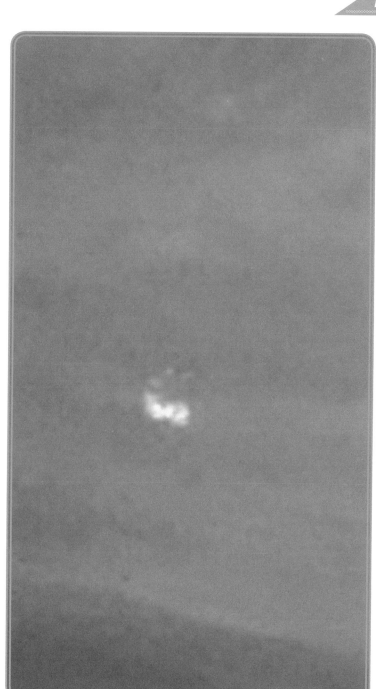

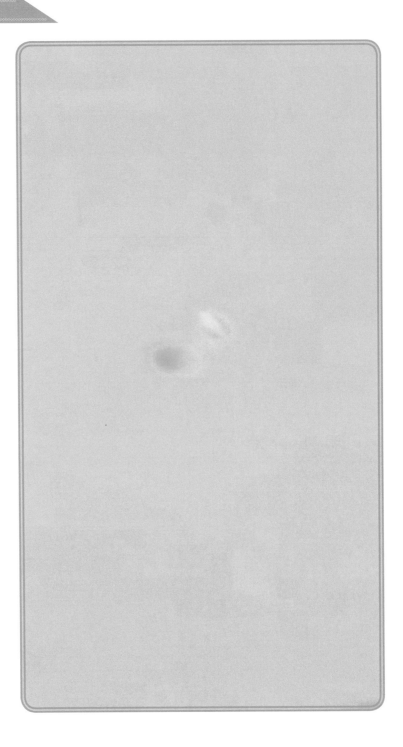

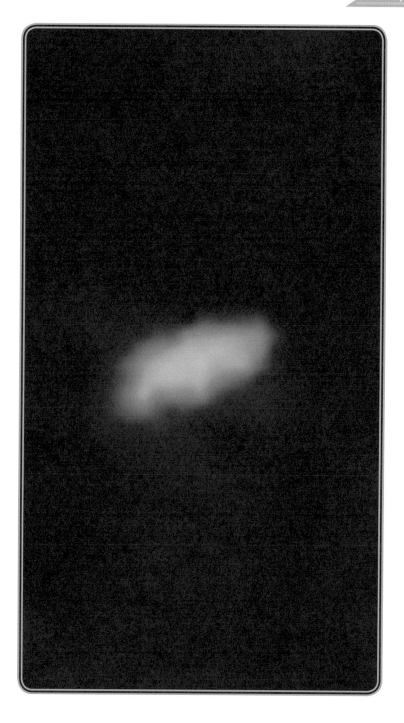

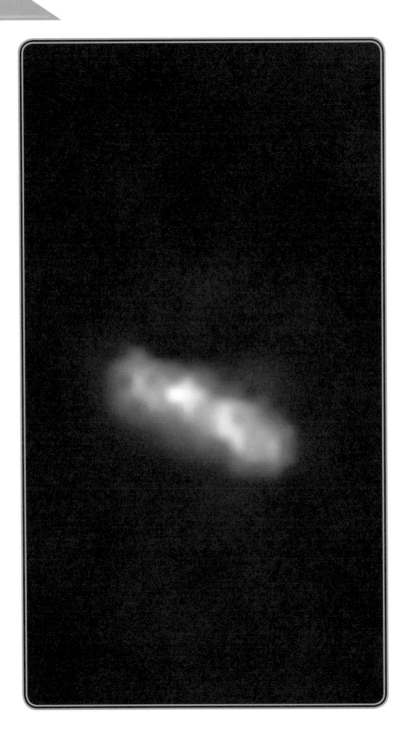

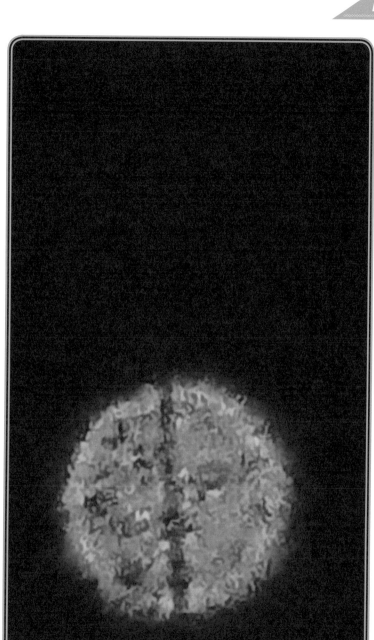

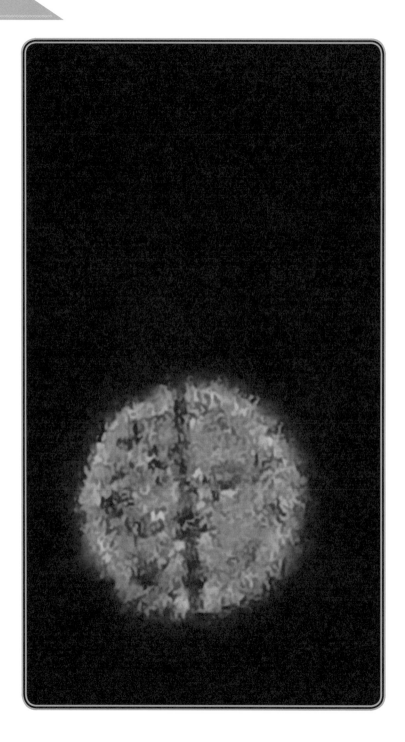

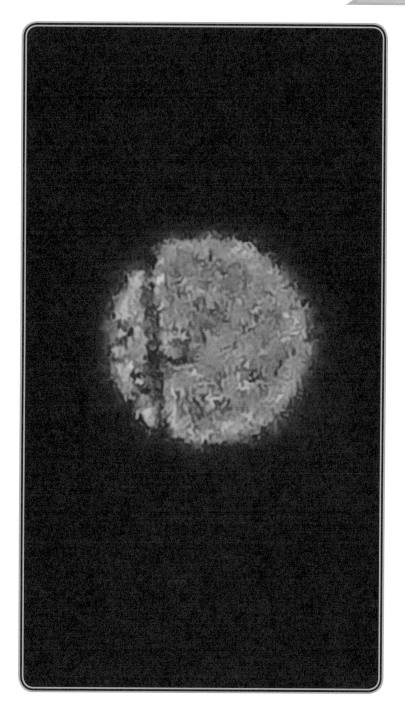

42

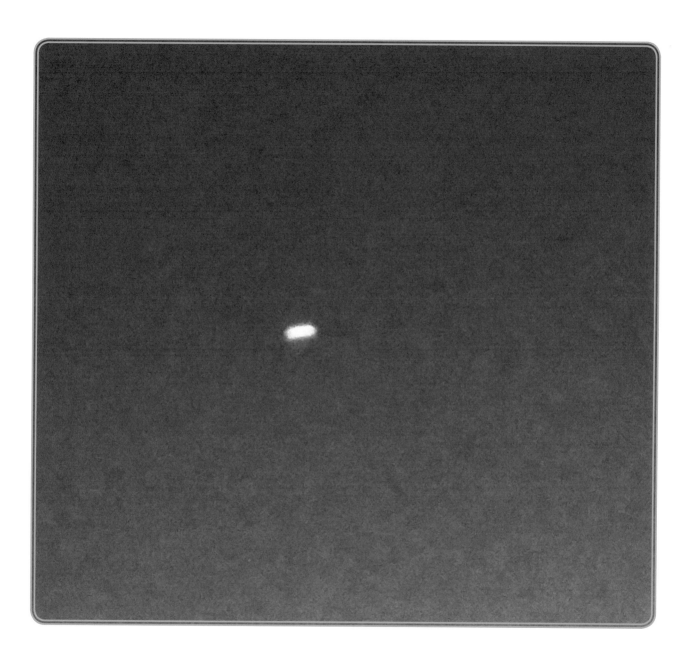

Slave

Knows no colors
For our endeavors
We all pay the elite
So we can eat
The cost of life
We give up our rights
To the people who have no souls
In order to fulfill their goals
Now we are all a slave
For all we gave

Written By:
William J.

Decades

0-10 growing and learning
11-20 becoming a young adult
21-30 figuring out who we are
31-40 family and career
41-50 knowledge of life
51-60 understanding of life
61-70 retirement staying busy
71-80 passing all your knowledge on
81-90 preparing for the transformation to next life

Peace

Is it just a dream
What does it Mean
That Everyone must get along
In order to belong
So we kill one another
To be like the others
What is the cost
For all the Lost?

Written by
William J.

Free Will

There are many sides of Heaven
Many depths of hell
All your deeds during life
Determine where you dwell
So stay positive, happy, and helpful to all
Who come into your life?
For we all share the same fate
To go into the light

Written by:
William J.

Life

It's a Long Journey
But a Short ride
It blinks, we say Bye
All the experiences we have
With Family and friends
That's what we remember
When we all meet the End!

Written by:
William J.

Printed in the United States
by Baker & Taylor Publisher Services